soups

RYLAND
PETERS
& SMALL

LONDON NEW YORK

soups

no-fuss recipes for hearty soups

Tonia George   photography by Yuki Sugiura

Dedicated to Jamie

Design and Photographic Art Direction Steve Painter
Editor Céline Hughes
Production Manager Patricia Harrington
Art Director Leslie Harrington
Publishing Director Alison Starling

Food Styling Tonia George
Prop Styling Tabitha Hawkins
Assistant Food Styling and Recipe Testing Georgie Footit
Indexer Hilary Bird

First published in the US in 2008
by Ryland Peters & Small, Inc.
519 Broadway, 5th Floor
New York, NY 10012
www.rylandpeters.com

10 9 8 7 6 5 4 3 2 1

Text © Tonia George 2008
Design and photographs
© Ryland Peters & Small 2008

ISBN 978 1 84597 730 6

Library of Congress Cataloging-in-Publication Data

George, Tonia.
  Soups : no-fuss recipes for hearty soups / Tonia George ; photography by
Yuki Sugiura.
      p. cm.
  Includes index.
  ISBN 978-1-84597-730-6
  1. Soups. I. Title.
  TX757.G46 2008
  641.8'13--dc22

2008018810

Printed and bound in China

Notes

• Eggs are large unless otherwise specified. Uncooked or partially cooked eggs should not be served to the very old, frail, young children, pregnant women, or those with compromised immune systems.

• All spoon measurements are level, unless otherwise specified.

• Ovens should be preheated to the specified temperature. Recipes in this book were tested using a regular oven. If using a convection oven, follow the manufacturer's instructions for adjusting temperatures.

contents

introduction

My love affair with soup was born while mourning the loss of my wisdom teeth. Besides satisfying the logistics of feeding a mouth that barely opened, soup proved its worth as a soothing elixir. For there is nothing more restorative than a bowl of soup—it's the culinary equivalent of a warm cuddle.

Pottering around my kitchen with pots bubbling on the stove under windows dripping with steam, I've learned a lot about what makes a good soup. First, texture is as important as flavor. Chunky soups keep the mind occupied with finding little treasures, while purées are pure comfort food.

Contrast in texture and flavor is imperative too. This is why a sweet, sticky pear, date and pine nut relish on a cauliflower soup, or a swirl of chile and rosemary oil atop a bowl of tomato soup works wonders. It's also why we love the crunch of fried croutons with a silky smooth potage.

As much as we purists love to lecture about the importance of a good stock, the truth is you can often get away with a good storebought broth. Stocks are thrifty by nature, so it's silly to go to the effort of making one especially. Stock-making needs to slot in with you; it should be made after a visit to the butcher, or after a roast. However, beefy French onion soup and a Thai broth bobbing with pork meatballs both call for the flavor of a homemade stock to underpin them.

Very few dishes evoke home and hearth quite so well as a bowl of steaming leek and potato soup. By contrast, soups from exotic climes are utterly transporting. A sip of garlicky monkfish bourride can stir up memories of sandy toes in the Nice sunshine. Either way, when the sky outside is gray, a bowl of hot soup provides the perfect antidote to winter.

chicken and meat

chicken stock

Light chicken stock provides a good background flavor for most soups. Brown stock requires the bones to be roasted until golden to give a more intense depth of flavor.

2¼ lb cooked chicken carcass (topped up with raw chicken wings, if desired)

1 onion, chopped

2 celery ribs, chopped

1 carrot, chopped

1 teaspoon black peppercorns

a few parsley sprigs or stalks

2 dried bay leaves

makes about 3 cups

For light stock, if using chicken wings, blanch in boiling water, then discard the water. Place the chicken carcass, all the other ingredients and 5 cups cold water in a large stockpot. Bring gently to a boil and cook for 2 hours. Taste and if not strong enough, strain and boil again until reduced and flavorful. Keep a large metal spoon nearby and skim off any scum. Let cool, then before chilling, skim off any fat. Refrigerate for 2 days or freeze for 3 months.

For brown stock, first roast the bones following the beef stock recipe below, then resume recipe above.

beef stock

Making your own beef stock is a labor of love, as getting hold of beef bones requires a visit to a friendly butcher. If I were to make it for one soup, it would be the French onion.

5 lb beef bones, such as ribs or shin

2 onions, chopped

2 carrots, chopped

1 leek, chopped

2 teaspoons black peppercorns

2 dried bay leaves

a few thyme sprigs

makes about 3 cups

Preheat the oven to 400°F. Roast the bones in a roasting pan for 30 minutes until golden. Transfer to a large stockpot and place the pan on the stovetop over high heat, add 1 cup water, scrape up any bits, and add to the pot. Pour over enough water to cover (about 1 quart), and bring to a boil. Skim off any scum, add the other ingredients, and simmer over low heat for 4 hours. Taste and if not strong enough, strain and boil for another 30 minutes until reduced. Strain again, preferably through a dampened, cheesecloth-lined sieve. Let cool, then before chilling, skim off any fat. Refrigerate for 3 days or freeze for 3 months.

Thai chicken, mushroom, and coconut soup

This is a classic Thai soup called *Tom Ka Gai*. It shouldn't sting the senses with chile, which is how some restaurants make it; it should soothe and warm and feel as though it is replenishing your energy. You can serve it without the rice noodles as an appetizer.

4 oz rice noodles

1⅔ cups coconut milk

¾ cup Light or Brown Chicken Stock (page 9)

2 lemon grass stalks, halved lengthwise and bruised

2 inches fresh galangal or ginger, peeled and sliced

5 kaffir lime leaves

3 tablespoons demerara sugar

2 tablespoons fish sauce

3 red bird's-eye chiles, bruised

6½ oz chicken breast or thigh, skinless and sliced into 1-inch strips

5 oz oyster mushrooms, halved

freshly squeezed juice of 1–2 limes

cilantro leaves, to serve

serves 4

Put the noodles in a bowl and cover with boiling water. Let soak for 20 minutes while you make the rest of the soup.

Put the coconut milk, stock, lemon grass, galangal, and lime leaves in a large saucepan and slowly bring to a boil over medium heat. Add the sugar, fish sauce, chiles, chicken, and mushrooms and simmer for 6–8 minutes until the chicken is cooked through. Stir in the lime juice and taste. If it needs more salt, add a dash of fish sauce and if it is hot and salty, it may need rounding off with a touch more sugar.

Drain the noodles and divide between 4 bowls. Ladle the soup over the noodles, garnish with the cilantro, and serve.

roast chicken, garlic, and watercress soup

You can either honor this soup by roasting a chicken especially for the occasion or you can buy a rotisserie chicken. Of course, if you've had a roast, providing you haven't picked every last bit of meat from it, it's a good way to use that up too. There's nothing more satisfying than two meals from one bird; it makes one feel very thrifty and clever.

a whole 2¾-lb chicken (small)

3 whole garlic bulbs

a 10-oz baking potato

2 tablespoons extra virgin olive oil, plus extra to serve

6 fresh thyme sprigs

4 cups Brown Chicken Stock (page 9)

5 oz watercress

sea salt and freshly ground black pepper

serves 4

Preheat the oven to 400°F.

Place the chicken in a roasting pan, wrap the garlic bulbs and potato in foil individually, and scatter around the edges. Drizzle the olive oil over the chicken, scatter the thyme sprigs over the top, and season well. Roast in the preheated oven for 1 hour.

Open the packages of roasted garlic and potato to allow them to cool off and at the same time check that they are really soft inside. If not, return to the oven for a little longer until soft. Pull the chicken meat from the carcass and keep the carcass for your next batch of chicken stock. Hopefully, you should have some chicken stock ready to go, but if not you can use the carcass to whip up a batch (see page 9).

Pour the stock into a large saucepan. Discard the skin from the potato, chop the flesh, and add it to the pan. Cut the tops off the garlic bulbs, squeeze out the soft flesh from inside the cloves, and add to the soup. Chop up the chicken meat and add that to the soup too. Transfer about a third of the soup to a blender along with the watercress and liquidize until smooth. Return to the pan and stir until blended. Add more water if you think it's too thick. Season to taste.

Divide the soup between 4 bowls and drizzle with extra olive oil.

chicken avgolemono

If you don't have any well-flavored chicken stock, then you should boil up a whole chicken to make the brown stock on page 9. Let cool, then reduce the stock and use it for this traditional Greek egg and lemon soup recipe along with the shredded meat from the carcass.

6 cups Light or Brown Chicken Stock (page 9)

½ cup long-grain rice

14 oz cooked chicken, shredded

3 eggs

freshly squeezed juice of 1 lemon

to serve

chopped fresh parsley

Fried Garlic Croutons (page 89)

serves 4

Heat the stock in a large saucepan and add the rice. Bring to a boil and simmer for 15 minutes or until the rice is tender. Add the chicken and warm through for 2–3 minutes.

In the meantime, whisk the eggs with the lemon juice in a small bowl. Add a ladleful of the warm stock and whisk until thinned. Remove the soup from the heat and gradually pour in the egg mixture, whisking to amalgamate it. It should thicken in the residual heat, but if you need to, place it over low heat for just 3–4 minutes, stirring the bottom of the pan to thicken. Do not return to high heat once the egg has been added, or it will boil and scramble.

Divide the soup between 4 bowls and garnish with parsley and Fried Garlic Croutons.

potato, bacon, and Savoy cabbage soup

This recipe was inspired by a soup called *zurek* that I often eat in a canteen where I work, which is run by Polish women. It's a Polish soup that uses a fermented flour batter. Instead of this, I have used some oatmeal, which is a little trick I picked up from the Scottish dish, mussel brose, and it thickens the soup up very nicely.

2 tablespoons extra virgin olive oil

8 thick slices of bacon, chopped

1 onion, chopped

2 garlic cloves, crushed

⅛ teaspoon ground allspice

10 oz potatoes, peeled and cubed

¼ Savoy cabbage, shredded

1⅔ cups Light Chicken Stock (page 9)

1⅔ cups whole milk

2 tablespoons fine oatmeal

freshly ground black pepper

serves 4

Heat the olive oil in a heavy-based saucepan or casserole dish and fry the bacon for 2–3 minutes, until cooked. Turn the heat down and add the onion and garlic. Cover and cook for 3 minutes, or until starting to soften.

Add the allspice and potatoes, cover, and cook for a further 2–3 minutes to start softening the potatoes. Add the cabbage and stir until it has wilted into the rest of the ingredients. Pour in the stock and milk and bring to a boil.

Mix the oatmeal with 3–4 tablespoons cold water until smooth and gradually whisk into the soup to thicken.

Divide the soup between 4 bowls and serve with a fresh grinding of black pepper.

split pea and sausage soup

Where does a casserole stop and a soup start? That question could certainly be asked in relation to this soup as it really seems to verge on a casserole. The thick wintry mix of tender lentils with chunks of sausage is so filling, it's perfect to get you ready for a long walk, or maybe just a long snooze on the couch.

2 tablespoons extra virgin olive oil

1 onion, chopped

1 leek, chopped

2 celery ribs, chopped

a pinch of grated nutmeg

1½ cups yellow split peas

6 cups Brown Chicken Stock (page 9)

2 dried bay leaves

8 oz sausages

sea salt and freshly ground black pepper

serves 6

Heat the olive oil in a large saucepan and cook the onion, leek, and celery gently over low heat for 8–10 minutes. Add the nutmeg and stir in. Add the split peas and mix into the vegetables. Add the stock and bay leaves, cover, and simmer for 45 minutes or until the peas are tender and beginning to get mushy when pressed with the back of a spoon.

Meanwhile, broil the sausages until cooked, then roughly chop. Add to the soup and cook for a further 10 minutes. Season to taste with sea salt and freshly ground pepper.

Divide the soup between 6 bowls, settle in front of a roaring fire, and enjoy.

pea and smoked ham soup with mint

Frozen or fresh peas make a very satisfying sweet and savory base for a soup. If you are into shelling your own peas from the garden, the results will be even better, but frozen peas pulled out of the freezer are just as good for a standby dinner. You could even get away with using dried mint too, if your fridge or garden is looking a bit bare.

3 tablespoons extra virgin olive oil, plus extra to serve

6 scallions, chopped

2 garlic cloves, sliced

6½ oz thick slices of smoked ham, finely chopped

a small handful of fresh mint, leaves only, or 1 teaspoon dried mint

1 lb peas (defrosted or fresh)

4 cups hot Brown Chicken Stock (page 9) or Vegetable Stock (page 47)

sea salt and freshly ground black pepper

serves 4

Heat the olive oil in a large saucepan over low heat and add the scallions. Cook for 2–3 minutes, then add the garlic, ham, and half the mint and cook for a further 2 minutes, stirring. Stir in the peas and pour in the hot stock. Simmer for 2–3 minutes until the peas are tender.

Transfer a third of the soup to a blender and liquidize until completely smooth. Pour back into the soup and mix until amalgamated. Season with just a little sea salt (the ham will be quite salty already) and some freshly ground black pepper. Add the remaining mint.

Divide the soup between 4 bowls and serve with a drizzle of olive oil and a fresh grinding of black pepper.

Thai pork and rice soup

I love these brothy soups which have a purity to them;
it makes them simple and complex at the same time.
I sometimes ring the changes with this combination and
make the meatballs into wontons if I happen to have some
wonton wrappers from the Asian grocers. Simply envelope
the meatballs in a triangle and then pinch the ends of the
wonton wrapper together. Or you could add a handful of
slippery noodles instead of the rice.

meatballs

3 garlic cloves, chopped

a small handful of cilantro,
leaves and roots

1 lb ground pork

2 teaspoons fish sauce

¼ teaspoon ground white
pepper

soup

5 cups Light Chicken Stock
(page 9)

1 inch fresh ginger, peeled
and shredded

1 teaspoon sugar

1 tablespoon fish sauce

1 cup shredded Chinese
cabbage

1 cup cooked short-grain rice
or 5 oz rice stick noodles

to serve

6 scallions, shredded

½ teaspoon sesame oil

serves 4

To make the meatballs, put the garlic and cilantro in
a food processor and blend together until chopped.
Add the pork, fish sauce, and pepper and process. Wet
your hands and roll the mixture into 1-inch meatballs.
Chill until needed.

To make the soup, heat the stock with the ginger,
sugar, and fish sauce and let it bubble for 5 minutes.
Lower in the pork meatballs and gently simmer for
3 minutes (the water should be barely bubbling).
Add the cabbage and rice and simmer for a further
2 minutes, or until the meatballs are cooked through.

Divide the soup between 4 bowls, scatter with
scallions, and drizzle with sesame oil.

parsnip, chorizo, and chestnut soup

This is a thick and unctuous soup; the kind you could wolf down after a long walk or building a snowman in the depths of winter. It's very heavy so a little goes a long way; I suggest you serve it as a meal in itself—offering it as an appetizer is likely to leave anyone too stuffed for a follow-up course.

4 oz chorizo, cubed

1 onion, chopped

3 garlic cloves, sliced

1 celery rib, chopped

1 carrot, chopped

3 parsnips, chopped

¼ teaspoon hot red pepper flakes

1 teaspoon ground cumin

6½ oz peeled, cooked chestnuts (fresh or vacuum-packed)

4 cups hot Light or Brown Chicken Stock (page 9) or ham stock

sea salt and freshly ground black pepper

serves 4–6

Put the chorizo in a large saucepan and heat gently for 2–3 minutes until the oil seeps out and the chorizo becomes slightly crispy. Lift out the chorizo with a slotted spoon, trying to leave as much oil behind as you can and set to one side.

Add the onion, garlic, celery, carrot, and parsnips to the pan, stir well, cover, and cook gently for 10 minutes, or until softening. Add the pepper flakes and cumin, season with sea salt and freshly ground black pepper, and stir to release the aroma. Add the chestnuts and hot stock, then cover and simmer over low heat for 25–30 minutes until everything is tender.

Transfer the contents of the pan to a blender (or use a handheld blender) and liquidize until smooth. Reheat the chorizo in a small skillet.

Divide the soup between 4–6 bowls and scatter with the crispy chorizo.

harrira

This is a soup sold all over Morocco. At Ramadan, when most of the country is fasting, there is an eerie silence in the usually bustling souks as stall vendors tuck into their harrira, their first meal of the day. It can be as rustic as you like but my version is defined by the subtle flavor of saffron and accompanying spices. Generally it has a little meat, tomatoes, and lots of spices. Some people stir in some egg at the end, or a fermented batter of flour and water, and I have even seen it with vermicelli and rice, but the way I like to make it, I find it thick enough without any of these.

2 tablespoons extra virgin olive oil

a 1-lb lamb shank

2 onions, sliced

3 celery ribs, chopped

3 garlic cloves, chopped

1 teaspoon ground cinnamon

½ teaspoon saffron threads

½ teaspoon ground ginger

several gratings of nutmeg

1 tablespoon tomato paste

4 tomatoes, chopped

2¾ cups lamb stock or water

14 oz canned chickpeas, drained and rinsed, or dried chickpeas soaked overnight

½ cup green lentils, rinsed

freshly squeezed juice of 1 lemon

2 tablespoons chopped fresh cilantro

sea salt and freshly ground black pepper

serves 4–6

Heat the olive oil in a heavy-based casserole dish, then add the lamb and brown evenly. Add the onions, celery, garlic, cinnamon, saffron, ginger, and nutmeg and season well. Turn the heat down a little, cover, and cook for 10 minutes until soft, stirring occasionally.

Stir in the tomato paste and the tomatoes and cook for a further 2–3 minutes. Add the stock, cover, and cook for 1 hour until the lamb is becoming tender.

Add the chickpeas and lentils and cook for a further 40 minutes until they are tender and the lamb can easily be pulled off the bone. Shred the meat from the shank, remove the bone, and discard. Add lemon juice to taste and check the seasoning (it needs quite a generous amount of salt). Stir in the cilantro.

Divide the soup between 4–6 bowls and tuck in.

Vietnamese beef pho

This is Vietnamese fast food—it's slurped down in a flash but be warned that it takes time to make. It's pronounced "fuh" and derives from the French *pot au feu* ("pot on fire"). It's a soothing, deeply flavored broth bobbing with slices of beef, rice noodles, and perky bean sprouts and served with a bowl of Thai basil, mint, chile, and lime which you add to your own taste. It is possibly one of the best dishes in the world.

1 tablespoon sunflower oil

1 star anise

2 lemon grass stalks, sliced

1 cinnamon stick

1 tablespoon coriander seeds

1 tablespoon black peppercorns

1¼ inches fresh ginger, sliced

4 garlic cloves, peeled and bruised

6 cups Beef Stock (page 9)

3 cilantro sprigs, roots included

5 oz rice noodles

¼ cup freshly squeezed lime juice

2 tablespoons fish sauce

6½ oz sirloin steak, thinly sliced

1 cup bean sprouts

3 shallots, thinly sliced

to serve

a handful of fresh Thai basil leaves

several fresh mint leaves

1 red chile, sliced

lime wedges

serves 4

First you must flavor your stock with all those lovely warming, fragrant flavors of Vietnam. Heat the sunflower oil in a large saucepan over low heat, then add the anise, lemon grass, cinnamon, coriander seeds, peppercorns, ginger, and garlic. Cook gently for 1–2 minutes to release their aromas. Pour in the stock and bring to a boil.

Add the cilantro sprigs and simmer for 30 minutes. Take off the heat and let infuse while you prepare the other ingredients.

Get ready a plate of condiments. Pile up the Thai basil, mint, chile, and lime wedges on a plate and keep in the fridge until you're ready.

When you're ready to eat, cook the rice noodles in a large pan of boiling water according to the manufacturer's instructions. Drain and refresh under cold running water. Divide between 4 bowls.

Strain the stock back into the pan and add enough lime juice and fish sauce to taste. Add the beef and cook for 1 minute, or until it is just cooked through. Ladle the beef and stock onto the noodles and scatter the bean sprouts and shallots over the top. Serve with the plate of condiments so everyone can season to taste.

beef, tamarind, and sweet potato soup

This soup is salty, sweet, meaty, and sour all at once. Beef brisket is perfect for this dish as it cooks down to meltingly tender flakes of deliciousness. All that red meat and stock is quite heavy and it needs the fresh herbs to perk up all the flavors. So just bear in mind that the garnish is not a frilly afterthought, but integral to the dish.

3 garlic cloves, peeled

2 shallots, chopped

2 green chiles, seeded and chopped

1 lb beef brisket or chuck

2 tablespoons peanut oil

6 cups hot Beef Stock (page 9)

¼ cup tamarind paste

4 kaffir lime leaves

2 sweet potatoes, peeled and cut into 1-inch chunks

5 oz egg noodles

1 tablespoon honey

sea salt

to serve

a handful of fresh mint and cilantro leaves

2 shallots, sliced

1 red chile, seeded and sliced

serves 4

Pound together the garlic, shallots, and chiles with a mortar and pestle or in a spice grinder.

Blanch the beef in a pan of boiling water for 1 minute, then drain. Rinse the beef to get rid of any impurities, then thinly slice.

Heat the peanut oil in a heavy-based casserole dish, then add the beef and brown evenly. Add the spice paste and toss for 1–2 minutes until fragrant, but don't allow it to burn. Add the beef stock, tamarind paste, and lime leaves and simmer for 2 hours until the beef is really tender.

Add the sweet potatoes and simmer for a further 30 minutes until tender. Season with honey and sea salt to taste.

Get ready a plate of condiments. Pile up the mint, cilantro, shallots, and chile on a plate and keep in the fridge until you're ready.

Divide the soup between 4 bowls. Serve with the plate of condiments so everyone can season to taste.

fish and seafood

fish stock

Fish stock only needs to simmer for 30 minutes to absorb the flavors. Bones, heads, and other unfriendly bits from white fish work the best. Salmon, sea bass, whiting, and hake are all good bets. For a deeper, sweeter flavor you can add shrimp shells to make a shellfish broth. This is perfect for the crab soup and any bisque recipes. Just discard anything bloody, such as the gills, as this will make the stock bitter.

1¼ lb fish bones

2 tablespoons extra virgin olive oil

1 onion, halved

1 celery rib

1 leek, chopped

1 teaspoon black peppercorns

a few fresh parsley sprigs or stalks

¾ cup white wine

makes 2½ cups

Rinse the fish bones under the tap. Heat the olive oil in a large stockpot and fry the bones for 5 minutes over gentle heat to bring out their flavor, but not to brown them.

Add the onion, celery, leek, peppercorns, parsley, and wine and bring to a boil to evaporate the wine. Pour over about 3¼ cups cold water, then bring back to a gentle simmer for 25 minutes, skimming off any impurities that have risen to the surface.

Strain through a dampened, cheesecloth-lined sieve. Let cool, then before chilling, remove any fat that has risen to the surface. Refrigerate for 1 day or freeze for 2 months.

monkfish, fennel, and saffron bourride

A bourride is a little like a bouillabaisse but thickened with a gorgeous, garlicky aïoli. My aïoli is spiced up with harissa and is heavenly spread on anything. I love making this soup for dinner parties, because it looks like you really know what you're doing and the toast, cheese, and aïoli get people involved and thinking about what they are eating.

3 tablespoons extra virgin olive oil

1 onion, chopped

1 fennel bulb, finely chopped

1 leek, white part sliced

10 oz new potatoes (unpeeled), thinly sliced

¼ teaspoon saffron threads

2 fresh thyme sprigs

2 large tomatoes, thinly sliced

20 oz monkfish fillets, skinned and sliced

4 cups Fish Stock (page 33)

toast, to serve

¾ cup grated Gruyère cheese, to serve

sea salt and freshly ground black pepper

aïoli

2 egg yolks

1 teaspoon Dijon mustard

¾ cup olive oil

2 garlic cloves, crushed

2 teaspoons harissa

1 tablespoon freshly squeezed lemon juice

Heat the olive oil in a large saucepan, then fry the onion, fennel, and leek over low heat for 5 minutes. Add the potatoes, saffron, and thyme, stirring once or twice, and cook until the potato starts to soften.

Add the tomatoes and monkfish in a layer on top and, without stirring, pour in the stock. It should come at least halfway up the fish; if not, top up with water. Bring to a boil over gentle heat with the lid on and cook for 10–12 minutes until the fish is cooked and the potatoes are tender.

Meanwhile, to make the aïoli, put the egg yolks and mustard in a medium mixing bowl and whisk with electric beaters. Trickle in the olive oil slowly, whisking until it emulsifies and thickens. Season with sea salt and freshly ground black pepper, then stir in the garlic, harissa, and lemon juice. Transfer half the aïoli to a serving dish.

Siphon off 2–3 ladlefuls of the liquid in the saucepan, add it to the remaining aïoli, and stir well until combined. Stir back into the saucepan. Warm over low heat and season to taste, but don't boil.

Divide the soup between 4–6 bowls and serve with toast, extra aïoli, and Gruyère.

serves 4–6

smoked haddock and bean soup

Smoked haddock provides that warm smoky flavor that cold wintry nights call for. I love beans in soups—they are so quick and easy to throw in and thicken soups up nicely. Here I've used both cannellini and butter beans.

¼ cup extra virgin olive oil

1 red onion, sliced

2½ cups Fish Stock (page 33)

3 dried bay leaves

finely grated zest of
1 unwaxed lemon

10 oz smoked haddock,
skinned and cubed

14 oz canned cannellini beans,
drained and rinsed

14 oz canned butter beans,
drained and rinsed

¼ cup crème fraîche or
sour cream

sea salt and freshly ground
black pepper

serves 4

Heat the olive oil in a large saucepan, then fry the onion. Cover and cook over low heat for 10 minutes, stirring every now and then until soft.

Pour in the stock, add the bay leaves and lemon zest, and bring to a gentle simmer. Add the smoked haddock and cook for 3–4 minutes until opaque. It will continue to cook in the residual heat too.

Liquidize half the cannellini and half the butter beans with ¾ cup water in a blender and stir into the soup. Stir in the remaining whole beans and the crème fraîche. Season with sea salt. If the soup is too thick, add enough water to thin it down.

Divide the soup between 4 bowls and serve with a fresh grinding of black pepper.

crab bisque

This soup is a very easy bisque to make that reminds me of those rust-hued Mediterranean soups that taste of shellfish and have a hint of hot pepper in them. You can of course buy, kill, and pick out the meat of your own crab but it's quite a performance, so I buy crabmeat (although that comes at a price, admittedly). If you want to make your fish stock more shellfishy, you could add some shrimp shells to the stock as well as the crab shells. The shrimp can be used in a sandwich the next day or even stirred into the bisque at the end.

1½ lb whole cooked Dungeness crab or 8 oz lump crabmeat

5 cups Fish Stock (page 33)

½ cup white wine

3 tablespoons butter

3 leeks, sliced

10 oz potatoes, peeled and diced

1 teaspoon tomato paste

3 tablespoons brandy

2 fresh tarragon sprigs

3 tablespoons heavy cream

¼ teaspoon ground mace

freshly squeezed juice of ½ lemon

a pinch of cayenne pepper, to serve

sea salt

serves 4

If using whole crab, prise out the white and brown crabmeat from its shell, place in a small bowl, and reserve. You should have at least 8 oz meat. Put the shell, stock, and wine in a saucepan and simmer for 20 minutes.

Heat the butter in a large skillet over low heat, then add the leeks. Cover and cook for 5 minutes until softened, but not browned. Add the potatoes and give it a good stir, then put the lid back on and cook for a further 5 minutes, giving it a stir every now and then to stop it from sticking. Add the tomato paste, brandy, and tarragon and turn up the heat to burn off the alcohol. Once it has evaporated, strain in half the stock mixture and simmer until the potatoes are completely soft, about 15 minutes.

Transfer the contents of the skillet to a blender and liquidize until smooth. Return to the skillet, strain in the remaining stock, then add the reserved crabmeat and the cream. Heat through and season to taste with sea salt, mace, and lemon juice.

Divide the soup between 4 bowls and serve sprinkled with cayenne pepper.

teriyaki mackerel and shiitake noodle soup

Japanese broths always feel like they are doing you the world of good. Shiitake mushrooms have that unique savory *umami* flavor to them that feels really satisfying. If you can't get hold of kombu (a Japanese seaweed sold dried in packets) and bonito flakes, you could use a fish stock mixed with miso soup.

6½ oz shiitake mushrooms, sliced

6½ oz udon noodles

3 oz baby spinach leaves

1 tablespoon light soy sauce

6 scallions, shredded and left in ice water to curl

teriyaki mackerel

3 tablespoons light soy sauce

2 tablespoons sake

2 teaspoons sugar

½ teaspoon freshly grated ginger

4 mackerel fillets

ginger dashi

6 inches kombu or
1 tablespoon instant dashi with bonito flakes

2 inches fresh ginger, peeled and thinly sliced

serves 4

To make the teriyaki, mix the soy sauce, sake, sugar, and ginger together in a shallow dish. Add the fish, toss well to coat in the teriyaki, and marinate for 15 minutes while you make the dashi.

To make the dashi, put the kombu and 1 quart water in a saucepan and gently heat, skimming off any scum. Just before it boils, remove and discard the kombu. Add the ginger to the water, bring to a boil, then strain though a fine sieve into a large saucepan. Alternatively, make up 3¼ cups instant dashi in a large saucepan. Add the shiitake mushrooms to the homemade or instant dashi and cook for 5 minutes or until softening.

Preheat the broiler.

Cook the noodles in a pan of water according to the manufacturer's instructions, drain, and run under cold water. Put the marinated fish on a broiler pan and broil for 3 minutes on each side until cooked through. Add the spinach to the dashi, along with the noodles.

Divide the soup between 4 bowls, season with soy sauce, and top with a piece of fish and the scallions.

shrimp tom yam

This soup never ceases to satisfy and just goes to show that flavor doesn't need to come from butter or cream. The end result is based on a good backbone of flavor that comes from a rich chicken stock. All the other aromatics need to be balanced against each other, so taste before serving and make any necessary adjustments.

1 quart Brown Chicken Stock (page 9)

1 lemon grass stalk, halved lengthwise and bruised

1 inch fresh ginger, peeled and thinly sliced

3 kaffir lime leaves

a small handful of cilantro, stalks finely chopped and leaves left whole

2 shallots, sliced

3 chiles, seeded and shredded

5 oz button mushrooms, halved

6½ oz uncooked jumbo shrimp, deveined and shelled but tails left intact

⅓ cup freshly squeezed lime juice

2 tablespoons sugar

¼ cup fish sauce

serves 4–6

Put the chicken stock in a large saucepan with the lemon grass, ginger, lime leaves, chopped cilantro stalks, shallots, chiles, and mushrooms. Bring to a boil, turn down the heat, and simmer for 10 minutes.

Butterfly the shrimp (cut down the back lengthwise with a sharp knife) and add them to the pan with the lime juice, sugar, and fish sauce and simmer for 1 minute or until the shrimp are pink. Scatter the reserved cilantro leaves into the soup. Take off the heat and taste, adding more fish sauce, lime juice, or sugar, as you see fit.

Divide the soup between 4–6 bowls and feel revived.

cacciucco with gremolata

This is an Italian seafood stew that begs for a big glass of wine and a hunk of ciabatta to accompany it. I sometimes like to toast a piece of bread and spoon the soup over this to bulk it out a bit. It's a great way of using up stale bread too, which in its soggy state tastes no different from fresh.

1 lb mussels, cleaned

2 tablespoons extra virgin olive oil

1 onion, chopped

2 carrots, cubed

2 celery ribs, chopped

4 garlic cloves, sliced

1 red chile, seeded and chopped

14 oz canned Italian plum tomatoes, chopped

1 teaspoon tomato paste

¾ cup white wine

2 dried bay leaves

4 cups Fish Stock (page 33)

1 lb sea bass fillets, cut into 2-inch pieces

6 uncooked jumbo shrimp

10 oz squid, cut into rings

gremolata

finely grated zest and freshly squeezed juice of 1 unwaxed lemon

1 tablespoon extra virgin olive oil

2 garlic cloves, chopped

2 tablespoons freshly chopped flatleaf parsley

serves 4

First prepare the mussels. Tap any unopen ones firmly on a worktop and if they do not close, discard them.

To make the gremolata, mix together the lemon zest, juice, olive oil, garlic, and parsley. Season well and set aside while you make the soup.

Heat the olive oil in a large saucepan and fry the onion, carrots, celery, and garlic for 8–10 minutes until softened. Add the chile, canned tomatoes, tomato paste, half the white wine, the bay leaves, and stock and bring to a boil.

Pour the remaining white wine into another pan and bring to a boil. Add the mussels, cover with a lid, and cook over high heat for 3–4 minutes until the shells open. Discard the cooking liquid and transfer the mussels to the soup pan. Discard any mussels that still have not opened. Add the fish and shrimp to the pan and simmer gently for 2–3 minutes or until cooked through. Add the squid and cook for 1 minute.

Divide the soup between 4 bowls and spoon over the gremolata.

vegetables

vegetable stock

Vegetable stock gives the least flavor in a soup—it is just a step up from flavored water. This is why generally I prefer to use chicken stock in soups, including vegetable soups. However, if you are vegetarian, you will find this much more useful and can use it as a substitute anywhere.

2 onions, chopped

3 carrots, chopped

3 celery ribs, chopped

2 leeks, chopped

1 dried bay leaf

1 fresh thyme sprig

½ teaspoon black peppercorns

a few parsley sprigs or stalks

makes 1 litre

Put all the ingredients in a stockpot and pour in 5 cups cold water. Bring to a gentle simmer and continue to cook for 2 hours. Keep a large metal spoon nearby and skim off any scum.

Taste and if not strong enough, strain and boil for another 30 minutes until reduced. Let cool, then before chilling, skim off any further scum. Refrigerate for 3 days or freeze for 3 months.

French onion soup

There aren't many ingredients in a French onion soup, so it follows that there aren't many places for mistakes to hide. Therefore you need to get the caramelization of the onions spot on—cook them slowly and then once soft, turn up the heat and cook until a sticky golden brown. The beef stock in this needs to be richly flavored or the soup will be insipid.

3 tablespoons butter

2¼ lb onions, sliced

2 garlic cloves, crushed

1 tablespoon sugar

2 tablespoons Cognac or brandy

1¼ cups hard apple cider

5 cups Beef Stock (page 9)

1 bouquet garni (1 sprig each of parsley, thyme, and bay)

sea salt and freshly ground black pepper

garlic toasts

¼ cup extra virgin olive oil

1 garlic clove, crushed

1 small baguette or ½ large baguette, sliced

2 cups grated Gruyère cheese

serves 4

Preheat the oven to 350°F.

To make the garlic toasts, mix the olive oil and garlic together and season well. Arrange the baguette slices on a baking sheet and brush with the garlic oil. Bake in the preheated oven for 25 minutes until crisp.

Melt the butter in a large saucepan or casserole dish over medium heat. Add the onions and garlic and stir until starting to soften. Turn the heat to low, cover, and cook gently for 25–30 minutes until really softened.

Take the lid off and add the sugar. Cook for a further 20 minutes, stirring until golden brown and extremely floppy-looking. This is the secret to a successful onion soup. Pour in the Cognac and cider and let bubble up for 1 minute. Add the stock and bouquet garni and stir to blend. Simmer for 45 minutes, then season to taste. Remove the bouquet garni.

Preheat the broiler.

Divide the soup between 4 ovenproof bowls and place them on a baking sheet. Float 2–3 garlic toasts on top of each bowl and scatter the Gruyère over the toasts. Broil until the Gruyère is bubbling and golden. Remove the baking sheet and lift off the hot bowls with an oven mitt, warning everyone that they are hot.

arugula soup with poached egg and truffle oil

If you love truffle oil, this is a great excuse to use some of that treasured bottle. If you don't, it is perfectly fine without it. In fact, the egg makes it a substantial meal by adding a bit of protein, but it would be fine without the egg too.

2 tablespoons butter

2 leeks, chopped

8 oz potatoes, peeled and chopped

4 cups Brown Chicken Stock (page 9)

6½ oz arugula

1 teaspoon white wine vinegar

4 eggs

6 tablespoons heavy cream

1–2 tablespoons truffle oil

sea salt and freshly ground black pepper

serves 4

Melt the butter in a large, heavy-based saucepan and add the leeks. Cover and cook over low heat for 8 minutes until softening and glistening. Add the potatoes and cook, covered, for a further 5 minutes. Pour in the stock and simmer for 15 minutes or until the potatoes are really tender. Remove from the heat and add the arugula, then let it wilt for 10 minutes.

Meanwhile, bring a deep skillet of water to a boil, add the vinegar, then turn down to a gentle simmer. Crack the eggs in each corner and turn off the heat. Let sit for 3 minutes.

Transfer the soup to a blender and liquidize until smooth. Return to the pan, stir in the cream, and season with sea salt and freshly ground black pepper.

Divide the soup between 4 bowls, top each with a poached egg, and serve with a fresh grinding of black pepper and a drizzle of truffle oil.

zucchini, fava bean, and lemon broth

This soup is very useful if you have a vegetable garden, as both zucchini and fava beans are easy to grow. It's also often the case that you end up with a real glut of them. To make the broth more substantial I sometimes add a scoop of risotto rice at the same time as the fava beans and a little more stock to compensate. If you are using large beans you might want to slip them out of their pale green jackets, but this is a real labor of love!

2 tablespoons extra virgin olive oil

1 unwaxed lemon

1 onion, chopped

3 tablespoons freshly chopped flatleaf parsley, plus extra to serve

1 lb zucchini, sliced

10 oz fava beans (shelled weight)

3¼ cups Light Chicken Stock (page 9) or Vegetable Stock (page 47)

Lemon and Thyme Oil (page 81), to serve

sea salt and freshly ground black pepper

serves 4

Heat the olive oil in a large saucepan. Peel the zest from the lemon in one large piece so it's easy to find later and add that to the pan. Add the onion, parsley, and zucchini, cover, and cook over low heat, stirring occasionally, for 8 minutes or until softening.

Remove the lemon zest. Add the fava beans and stock, season well, and return to the heat for a further 20 minutes.

Transfer a quarter of the soup to a blender, liquidize until smooth, then stir back into the soup. Check the seasoning and add lemon juice to taste.

Divide the soup between 4 bowls, drizzle with Lemon and Thyme Oil, and serve with extra parsley and a fresh grinding of black pepper.

tomato soup

The trick with tomato soup is to get a bit of acidity fighting back against the natural sweetness of the tomato. So first and foremost you need sweet tomatoes, but to be sure you can add some brown sugar to compensate—it's up to you to decide how much. The vinegar will then cut through this sweetness. I've had to restrain myself and not add chile as I'm running the risk of becoming a compulsive chile consumer. If you are less guilt-ridden you can add a chopped red chile to the onion, which will go down very nicely indeed.

2 red onions, chopped

3 garlic cloves, crushed

¼ cup extra virgin olive oil

5 lb plum tomatoes, roughly chopped

1–2 tablespoons soft light brown sugar

2 tablespoons red wine vinegar

3 cups Vegetable Stock (page 47)

Chile and Rosemary Oil (page 81), to serve

sea salt and freshly ground black pepper

serves 4

Put the onions, garlic, and olive oil in a large saucepan, cover, and cook over low heat for 10 minutes, stirring occasionally until soft. Do not let it brown.

Add the tomatoes, sugar, vinegar, and stock and season well. Bring to a boil, then turn down the heat and simmer for 30 minutes, stirring occasionally.

Transfer to a blender in batches and liquidize until really smooth.

Divide the soup between 4 bowls and drizzle with Chile and Rosemary Oil.

leek and potato soup

Sometimes the classics are the best, and with leek and potato this is certainly true. If you are using nice clean leeks, you can slice them lengthwise and simply rinse them under the faucet, but if you are lucky enough to have some from the garden complete with the mud and insects that cohabit with them, place them in a sink full of warm water and swirl them around to dissolve the mud and encourage it to come out.

3 tablespoons butter

4 leeks (about 1 lb), chopped

3 potatoes, peeled and chopped (about 8 oz)

1 onion, finely chopped

2 cups Vegetable Stock (page 47)

1¼ cups milk

2 dried bay leaves

2 tablespoons freshly snipped chives, to serve

Goat Cheese and Anchovy Palmiers (page 86), optional

sea salt and freshly ground black pepper

serves 4–6

Melt the butter in a large, preferably heavy-based saucepan and add the leeks, potatoes, onion, and a large pinch of salt. Cover and cook over low heat for 15 minutes until soft and translucent. Stir occasionally so that the vegetables don't catch.

Add the stock, milk, and bay leaves and bring to a boil. Turn the heat down and simmer, covered, for 20 minutes until the potato is so soft it is falling apart.

Transfer the soup to a blender, removing the bay leaves as you unearth them, and liquidize until smooth. Strain the blended soup back into the pan to get it extra smooth. Bring back to a boil.

Divide the soup between 4–6 bowls and scatter with chives and a fresh grinding of black pepper. Serve with Goat Cheese and Anchovy Palmiers, if desired.

corn and pancetta chowder

A chowder normally contains fish and is reputed to have come from the large cauldrons found on fishermen's boats called *chaudières*. Nowadays corn replaces the fish in New England, but the principle is still the same—a creamy stock thickened with potatoes and spiked with the rich flavor of smoky bacon.

3 tablespoons butter

5 oz pancetta, cubed

1 onion, sliced

2 carrots, finely chopped

10 oz new potatoes (unpeeled), thinly sliced

2 tablespoons flour

2½ cups whole milk

1⅔ cups Light or Brown Chicken Stock (page 9) or Vegetable Stock (page 47)

3 dried bay leaves

2½ cups corn kernels (thawed if frozen)

3 tablespoons heavy cream

sea salt and freshly ground black pepper

serves 4

Heat the butter in a large saucepan and fry the pancetta until crisp. Add the onion, carrots, and potatoes, cover, and cook gently for 15–20 minutes until soft. Stir occasionally.

Sprinkle the flour into the pan and cook for 1 minute, stirring it into the vegetables. Pour in the milk gradually, blending it with the flour, then add the stock and bay leaves; bring to a gentle simmer. Add the corn and cook for 5 minutes.

Remove from the heat, stir in the cream, and season with sea salt.

Divide the soup between 4 bowls and serve with a fresh grinding of black pepper

minestrone with Parmesan rind

I like to add cured pork in its many guises to most things vegetarian, which I realize is slightly controversial. You see, I adore vegetables, but I just find they taste better with a little fried bacon or pancetta. If you don't eat meat, there is one trick I can offer instead. Buy your Parmesan in a big chunk and hang on to the rinds in an airtight container in the fridge. Use them for soups like this that need a strong undercurrent; they will add a similar depth of flavor and saltiness.

¼ cup extra virgin olive oil, plus extra to serve

2 carrots, chopped

1 red onion, chopped

4 celery ribs, diced and leaves reserved

6 garlic cloves, sliced

2 tablespoons freshly chopped flatleaf parsley

2 teaspoons tomato paste

14 oz canned Italian plum tomatoes, chopped

4 cups hot Brown Chicken Stock (page 9) or Vegetable Stock (page 47)

14 oz canned borlotti beans, drained and rinsed

Parmesan rind (optional)

5 oz cavolo nero or spring greens, shredded

3½ oz spaghetti, broken up

grated Parmesan, to serve

sea salt and freshly ground black pepper

serves 4–6

Heat the olive oil in a large, heavy-based saucepan, then add the carrots, onion, celery, and garlic. Cover and cook very slowly over low heat, stirring occasionally, until thoroughly softened.

Add the parsley, tomato paste, and canned tomatoes and cook for 5 minutes. Pour in the stock and borlotti beans and bring to a boil. If using a Parmesan rind, add this now. Once boiling, add the cavolo nero and simmer for 20 minutes.

Add the spaghetti and cook for 2–3 minutes less than the manufacturer's instructions suggest (by the time you have ladled it into bowls it will be perfectly cooked). Taste and add seasoning if it needs it.

Divide the soup between 4–6 bowls and drizzle with extra olive oil. Serve with a bowl of grated Parmesan to sprinkle over the top.

chilled avocado soup with cilantro

You won't be able to eat a huge amount of this soup as it is very rich and you can have too much of a good thing. I sometimes like to serve it in small glasses with a broiled chicken tender resting on the top. The only stipulation here is that the avocados must be ripe and yielding or you won't get that nutty, creamy flavor they are so admired for.

2 tablespoons avocado oil or extra virgin olive oil, plus extra to serve

2 garlic cloves, crushed

1 red chile, seeded and chopped

½ teaspoon ground cumin

4 scallions, chopped

2 large tomatoes, peeled, seeded, and chopped

2 ripe avocados, halved and pitted

¼ cup Greek yogurt

2¾ cups chilled Vegetable Stock (page 47) or Light Chicken Stock (page 9)

freshly squeezed juice of 3 limes

a small handful of cilantro leaves

Red Pepper and Cilantro Relish (page 82), to serve

sea salt and freshly ground black pepper

serves 4–6

Put the oil, garlic, chile, cumin, and scallions in a skillet over medium heat and cook for 1 minute. Add the tomatoes and cook for about 3–4 minutes until you have a thick paste, then let cool slightly.

Transfer the contents of the skillet to a blender and whizz with a pinch of salt until finely chopped. Scoop out the flesh of the avocados and add to the blender along with the yogurt. Liquidize until smooth. Add the chicken stock, lime juice, and cilantro and liquidize again. Season to taste.

Divide the soup between 4–6 bowls and drizzle with Red Pepper and Cilantro Relish and a little extra oil.

gazpacho

1 oz stale white bread, crusts removed

¼ red onion, chopped

3 garlic cloves, crushed

2¼ lb ripe tomatoes, quartered

1 red bell pepper, seeded and chopped

¼ cucumber, finely chopped

3 tablespoons sherry vinegar

6 tablespoons extra virgin olive oil

a few drops of Tabasco

sea salt and freshly ground black pepper

serves 6

You really need sweet-smelling tomatoes for this soup or you won't have the strength of flavor that you need in a gazpacho.

Put the bread in a food processor and blend until you have crumbs, then tip into a bowl and set aside.

Fix the bowl back on the processor, add the onion and garlic, and blend until chopped. Add the tomatoes and bell pepper and blend until puréed. Tip out and stir in the remaining ingredients, adding a little water if it is too thick. Season generously and chill for 2 hours.

Serve icy cold in shot glasses.

chilled cucumber soup

1 cucumber, peeled

2 tablespoons freshly chopped dill

1 tablespoon freshly chopped mint

1 small garlic clove, crushed

freshly squeezed juice of 1 lemon

6 tablespoons plain yogurt

¼ cup extra virgin olive oil

sea salt and freshly ground black pepper

serves 4

This is a refreshing palate cleanser that is perfect as a starter. It also makes a swish canapé served in a dinky shot glass. It might sound bland and all too easy when you read the recipe, but the cucumber has an acidic kick that gets your appetite going.

Put the cucumber, herbs, and garlic in a food processor and whizz for 1 minute until puréed. Add the lemon juice, yogurt, and olive oil and blend again. Season to taste. Chill for 2 hours.

Serve icy cold in shot glasses.

lentil, spinach, and cumin soup

This is Lebanese in origin, but soups like this are served all over the Middle East. Crispy fried onions are a lovely topping, but you have to be brave and really brown them so they look dare I say it, almost black. In order to do this without burning them, you have to really soften them to start with.

3 tablespoons extra virgin olive oil

2 onions, sliced

4 garlic cloves, sliced

1 teaspoon ground coriander

1 teaspoon cumin seeds

¾ cup brown or green lentils

5 cups Vegetable Stock (page 47)

6½ cups spinach

freshly squeezed juice of 1 lemon

sea salt and freshly ground black pepper

to serve

¼ cup Greek yogurt

¼ cup pine nuts, lightly toasted

serves 4

Heat the olive oil in a large, heavy-based saucepan and add the onions. Cook, covered, for 8–10 minutes until softened. Remove half the onion and set aside.

Continue to cook the onion left in the pan for a further 10 minutes until deep brown, sweet, and caramelized. Take out and set aside for the garnish.

Return the softened onion to the pan and add the garlic, coriander, cumin seeds, and lentils and stir for 1–2 minutes until well coated in oil. Add the stock, bring to a boil, then turn down to a gentle simmer for 30 minutes until the lentils are lovely and soft.

Add the spinach and stir until wilted. Transfer half the soup to a blender and liquidize until you have a purée. Stir back into the soup. Season with lemon juice, sea salt, and freshly ground black pepper.

Divide the soup between 4 bowls, add a dollop of Greek yogurt, and scatter the pine nuts and fried onions over the top.

roast eggplant, red bell pepper, and oregano soup

This may look like just another tomato soup, but the smoky flavors of the roasted eggplant and red bell peppers make it really enticing. Oregano is a perfect match to all these flavors with its woody aroma, and yes the soup really does need all that roasted garlic!

1 large eggplant

4 red bell peppers

2 fresh thyme sprigs

1 garlic bulb, halved horizontally

2 tablespoons extra virgin olive oil

1 red onion, cut into wedges

2 cups Vegetable Stock (page 47)

1¼ cups passata or tomato purée

a handful of fresh oregano leaves

sea salt and freshly ground black pepper

to serve

Basil Oil (page 81)

fresh basil leaves

serves 4–6

Preheat the oven to 375°F.

Put the whole eggplant and bell peppers in a large roasting pan. Sandwich the thyme between the garlic halves, drizzle with the olive oil, then wrap in aluminum foil and add to the pan. Roast in the preheated oven for 35 minutes.

Remove the garlic from the oven, checking it is tender first, and set aside to cool. Remove the bell peppers, transfer to a freezer bag, seal, and let cool.

Add the onion to the roasting pan (still containing the eggplant) and roast for 20 minutes or until the eggplant feels tender when pierced with a knife.

Meanwhile, peel the skins off the cooled peppers and discard. Transfer the flesh to a blender and liquidize with a third of the stock until smooth. Transfer to a saucepan. Squeeze out the soft flesh from inside the garlic cloves and add to the blender. Spoon the flesh of the eggplant into the blender with the onion and another third of the stock. Blend until smooth, then add to the pepper purée in the saucepan. Add the passata, oregano, and remaining stock and bring to a boil. Season to taste.

Divide the soup between 4–6 bowls, scatter with basil leaves, and drizzle with Basil Oil.

spiced pumpkin and coconut soup

Pumpkins are tricky beasts to handle with their almost impenetrable flesh and skin. The best way to tackle one is to place it on a work surface and, keeping your hands well clear, hack into it with a large, sharp knife—in the manner of a slightly crazed butcher. First split it in half, then once you have a flat side, you can put it on a cutting board and slice it into large chunks. Peel with an upright peeler and chop the flesh. Use a butternut squash if pumpkins aren't available.

2¼ lb pumpkin or butternut squash, peeled, seeded, and cut into 1-inch cubes

1 onion, cut into wedges

½ teaspoon red pepper flakes

1 teaspoon ground coriander

1 teaspoon ground ginger

¼ cup extra virgin olive oil

3 whole garlic cloves, peeled

3¼ cups Light or Brown Chicken Stock (page 9)

6 tablespoons coconut milk

2 tablespoons fish sauce

freshly squeezed juice of 1 lime

freshly ground black pepper

to serve

heavy cream, to serve

chopped red chiles, to serve (optional)

serves 4–6

Preheat the oven to 400°F.

Put the pumpkin, onion, pepper flakes, coriander, ginger, and olive oil in a large roasting pan and toss well. Cover with aluminum foil and roast in the preheated oven for 40 minutes, stirring halfway through, until almost soft.

Remove the foil and discard, add the garlic cloves, and return to the oven for a further 20 minutes or until the garlic is tender.

When the pumpkin is soft, transfer the contents of the roasting pan to a blender (or use a handheld blender) and liquidize with half the stock until smooth. Return to the pan and add the remaining stock and the coconut milk. Bring to a boil and simmer for about 10 minutes to allow the flavors to mingle. Stir in the fish sauce and lime juice and taste for seasoning—if it needs more salt, add a dash more fish sauce.

Divide the soup between 4–6 bowls, drizzle with cream, and finish with a fresh grinding of black pepper or some chopped red chiles.

Turkish leek, barley, and yogurt soup

Hot yogurt soups are often made with rice but I like them with pearl barley and found a recipe that does the same by Claudia Roden, a fount of knowledge for all things Levant. The yogurt can be unstable and is often mixed with egg and flour to stabilize it, but I find if you don't heat it too much it shouldn't curdle.

2 tablespoons butter

1 onion, finely chopped

3 leeks, thinly sliced

2 green chiles, seeded and chopped

1 tablespoon flour

⅔ cup pearl barley

5 cups Light or Brown Chicken Stock (page 9)

1 cinnamon stick

6½ oz Greek yogurt

freshly squeezed juice of ½ lemon

Paprika, Mint, and Lemon Butter (page 85), to serve

sea salt and freshly ground black pepper

serves 4

Melt the butter in a large, heavy-based saucepan and sauté the onion, leeks, and chiles, covered, over low/medium heat for 10 minutes until softening. Stir occasionally so they don't catch or brown.

Add the flour and barley and stir around for 1 minute to toast slightly. Add the stock and cinnamon stick. Simmer for a further 30 minutes, until the barley is lovely and tender.

Remove the pan from the heat. In a separate bowl, beat the yogurt and lemon juice with a ladleful of the liquid from the pan. Add this to the soup, beating it in, and return to a low heat. Cook, stirring, for just 2–3 minutes until warmed through, but don't let it boil.

Meanwhile, heat a skillet and melt the Paprika, Mint, and Lemon Butter until it starts to froth and continue to cook until golden.

Divide the soup between 4 bowls and spoon the Paprika, Mint, and Lemon Butter over the top.

cauliflower and Stilton soup

Cauliflower has a gentle spiciness and creaminess that make for wonderful soups. The Stilton can be replaced with Gorgonzola or Roquefort if you prefer. The Pear, Date, and Pine Nut Relish is a lovely touch, so if you can make it in advance of the soup then I would urge you to do so.

1 cauliflower (about 20 oz)

4 cups Vegetable Stock (page 47) or Light or Brown Chicken Stock (page 9)

2 tablespoons butter

1 onion, chopped

2 celery ribs, chopped

1 leek, chopped

4 fresh thyme sprigs, leaves only

4 dried bay leaves

5 oz Stilton

⅓ cup crème fraîche or heavy cream

Pear, Date, and Pine Nut Relish (page 83), to serve

sea salt and freshly ground black pepper

serves 4

Pull the outer leaves off the cauliflower, cut off the stem, and chop it up. Put these bits into a large saucepan with the stock. Bring to a boil and simmer until ready to use. Chop or break the cauliflower florets into 2-inch pieces.

Melt the butter in another large saucepan and cook the onion, celery, and leek, covered, over low heat for 10–15 minutes until soft but not colored.

Add the cauliflower florets, thyme, bay leaves, and seasoning. Strain the stock into the pan, discarding the bits and simmer for a further 20–25 minutes until the cauliflower is very soft.

Transfer the contents of the pan, in batches, to a blender and liquidize until smooth, returning each batch back to the pan in which you cooked the stock. Place over low heat and add the Stilton and crème fraîche. Heat, stirring, until melted. Season to taste.

Divide the soup between 4 bowls and spoon the Pear, Date, and Pine Nut Relish over the top.

spiced carrot soup

The delicate flavor of carrots is best blended with vegetable stock or water as chicken muddies the flavor of really good carrots. However, if you're doubtful of your carrots' flavor, go for a good chicken stock.

3 tablespoons butter

1 onion, chopped

1¾ lb carrots, chopped

2 teaspoons ground coriander

½ teaspoon ground ginger

¼ teaspoon ground red pepper

4 cups Vegetable Stock (page 47) or water

4 tablespoons heavy cream

2 tablespoons sunflower oil

2 inches fresh ginger, cut into matchsticks

Garlic, Cilantro, and Lime Butter (page 84), melted, to serve

sea salt and freshly ground black pepper

serves 4

Melt the butter in a large saucepan and sauté the onion for 5–8 minutes until softened. Add the carrots, coriander, ground ginger, and red pepper and stir into the butter to coat them and release the flavor of the spices. Season well, then pour in the stock. Simmer for 40 minutes.

Transfer the contents of the pan to a blender in batches (or use a handheld blender) and liquidize to a smooth purée. Stir in the cream. Add a little more water if it is too thick and season to taste.

Heat the sunflower oil in a skillet over high heat and fry the fresh ginger for 1 minute, or until crisp.

Divide the soup between 4 bowls and garnish with the ginger and some Garlic, Cilantro, and Lime Butter.

mushroom soup with Madeira and hazelnuts

Mushrooms and their earthiness blend really well with the sweet, mellow tang of Madeira wine. The toasted hazelnuts add a lovely thickness to the soup and another complimentary flavor, but you can omit them if you prefer.

3 tablespoons butter

1 large onion, chopped

3 garlic cloves, crushed

3 tablespoons blanched hazelnuts

3 tablespoons freshly chopped parsley

12 oz brown mushrooms, sliced

1 oz dried porcini mushrooms

6 tablespoons Madeira

4 cups hot Vegetable Stock (page 47) or Light Chicken Stock (page 9)

serves 4–6

Melt the butter in a large saucepan and add the onion and garlic. Cover and cook over low heat for 10 minutes, or until soft. Stir occasionally so that they don't color. Meanwhile, toast the hazelnuts in a dry skillet and roughly chop, then set aside.

Add half the parsley and all the mushrooms to the saucepan and turn the heat up to medium. Cover and cook, stirring, for 15 minutes until they are softened.

Put the dried mushrooms in a heatproof bowl with ½ cup of the hot stock and set aside to soak for about 15 minutes to rehydrate.

Add the Madeira to the pan and cook until it evaporates. Add the remaining stock and the dried mushrooms with their soaking liquid, cover, and cook for 10 minutes.

Transfer half the soup to a blender, along with half the hazelnuts and liquidize until smooth, then stir back into the pan and heat through.

Divide the soup between 4–6 bowls and scatter the remaining parsley and toasted hazelnuts over the top.

accompaniments

flavored oils

basil oil

This bright green, sludgy oil is especially good with any tomato-based soup.

1 cup packed fresh basil leaves

1 small garlic clove, chopped

¾ cup extra virgin olive oil

makes ¾ cup

Put the basil, garlic, a large pinch of salt, and some freshly ground black pepper in a food processor. Blend until roughly chopped. With the motor running, gradually trickle in the olive oil until it is blended. Transfer to a clean, lidded jar, seal, and chill for up to 1 week.

chile and rosemary oil

This is good with seafood soups or any mild soup that needs a warm kick to it. It gets stronger the longer you leave it.

2 fresh rosemary sprigs

⅔ cup extra virgin olive oil

3 large red chiles, seeded and finely chopped

makes ⅔ cup

Put the rosemary and olive oil in a small saucepan and heat gently for 5 minutes. Remove from the heat, add the chiles, and let cool. Season to taste. Transfer to a clean, lidded jar, seal, and chill for up to 2 days.

lemon and thyme oil

This lemony oil works well when you want a bit of an acidic bite added to your soup.

2 unwaxed lemons

2 fresh thyme or lemon thyme sprigs

1 cup extra virgin olive oil

makes 1 cup

Peel off the lemon zest using a potato peeler, making sure you leave behind the bitter white pith. Put the lemon zest, thyme, and olive oil in a small saucepan and heat gently for 10 minutes. Remove from the heat and let cool. Season to taste. Transfer to a clean, lidded jar, seal, and chill for up to 2–3 days.

simple relishes

These are four simple relishes that are lovely on soups, where their freshness contrasts against sometimes heavy vegetables. They get a bit lost on chunky soups so I tend to use them for the puréed varieties.

tomato, chive, and red onion relish

3 plum tomatoes, seeded and finely chopped

1 tablespoon snipped chives

½ red onion, finely chopped

1 small garlic clove, crushed

3 tablespoons extra virgin olive oil

makes about 1 cup

Combine all the ingredients in a bowl and season to taste.

red pepper and cilantro relish

½ red bell pepper, seeded and finely chopped

2 tablespoons freshly chopped cilantro

2 scallions, sliced

freshly squeezed juice of 1 lime

1 tablespoon extra virgin olive oil

makes about 1 cup

Combine all the ingredients in a bowl and season to taste.

preserved lemon and olive relish

1 large or 3 small preserved lemons

⅓ cup pitted green olives, chopped

2 tablespoons extra virgin olive oil

2 tablespoons freshly chopped flatleaf parsley

½ teaspoon paprika

makes about ¾ cup

Halve the preserved lemons. Scoop out the flesh and discard. Finely chop the skin and place in a bowl. Stir in the olives, olive oil, and parsley (don't add any salt as the lemons are salty enough). Sprinkle the paprika over the top.

pear, date, and pine nut relish

2 tablespoons butter

3 tablespoons pine nuts

2 pears, peeled, cored, and cut into ¾-inch cubes

3 Medjool dates, finely chopped

⅓ cup cider vinegar

2 tablespoons brown sugar

makes about 1¼ cups

Melt the butter in a saucepan over medium heat and add the pine nuts. Cook, stirring, for about 2 minutes or until golden. Add the pears, cover, and cook for 2–3 minutes until softening. Add the dates, vinegar, and sugar, season, and cook for 10–15 minutes, uncovered, until the liquid has evaporated (add a splash of water if it dries out too fast). Let cool a little before serving.

flavored butters

These butters only take 10 minutes to whip together, if you remember to leave the butter out to soften! They'll make a fair bit, which you can freeze for up to 6 weeks and use on soups, simple broiled chicken, or steak suppers.

garlic, cilantro, and lime butter

6½ tablepoons butter, softened

1 garlic clove, crushed

¼ cup freshly chopped cilantro

finely grated zest of 2 unwaxed limes and freshly squeezed juice of 1

makes 1 stick

Beat the butter in a mixing bowl with a wooden spoon until light and fluffy. Add the garlic, cilantro, and lime zest and juice and season well. Beat together until everything is combined. Using a spatula, scoop out the butter and place on an 8-inch square of waxed paper. Roll up into a sausage, twist the ends, and chill for 1 hour. Slice off rounds or melt and drizzle over your hot soup.

paprika, mint, and lemon butter

10 tablespoons butter, softened

1 garlic clove, crushed

1 teaspoon paprika

¼–½ teaspoon red pepper flakes

2 tablespoons freshly chopped mint

2 scallions, finely chopped

finely grated zest of 1 unwaxed lemon and freshly squeezed juice of ½

makes 1½ sticks

Beat the butter in a mixing bowl with a wooden spoon until light and fluffy. Add the garlic, paprika, pepper flakes, mint, scallions, lemon zest, and juice and season well. Beat together until everything is combined. Using a spatula, scoop out the butter and place on an 8-inch square of waxed paper. Roll up into a sausage, twist the ends, and chill for 1 hour. Slice off rounds or melt and drizzle over your hot soup.

goat cheese and anchovy palmiers

These adorable little pastries are a take on the sweet pastries you often find in Spain, which are made in the same manner except with sugar. I love the salty bite the cheese and anchovies give them, but they are ridiculously addictive.

a 1-lb package puff pastry, thawed if frozen

3½ oz goat cheese spread or crumbled soft goat cheese

1¾ oz canned anchovies, drained and chopped

2 tablespoons freshly chopped thyme

makes 32

Preheat the oven to 400°F.

Cut the pastry in half. Take one half and put it on a lightly floured surface. Roll out into a rectangle approximately 8 x 12 inches. Spread with half the goat cheese and scatter with half the anchovies and thyme. Repeat this process with the other piece of pastry. Roll the shorter sides very tightly into the center and squash together tightly. Cut into slices about ¾ inch thick and place on 2 baking sheets. Flatten each one well with the palm of your hand. Bake in the preheated oven for 20–25 minutes until golden. Let cool on the baking sheets.

tapenade and Parmesan cheese straws

If you like, you can spread these with pesto or sun-dried tomato paste instead of the tapenade, and you can vary the cheese too. Or simply brush with butter and scatter with sesame or poppy seeds. They need eating up within a day or two after which they lose their appeal.

1 egg, beaten

2 tablespoons whole milk

a 12-oz package puff pastry, thawed if frozen

¾ cup finely grated Parmesan

3 tablespoons black olive tapenade

makes 15

Preheat the oven to 400°F.

Mix the egg with the milk. Cut the pastry in half. Take one half and put it on a lightly floured surface. Roll out into a 12-inch square. Repeat with the other half. Brush one sheet with egg wash. Scatter with two-thirds of the Parmesan. Spread the other sheet with tapenade and place on top of the first sheet, spread-side down. Press gently and glaze again with the remaining egg wash. Cut into ½-inch strips, twist several times, and transfer to 2 baking sheets. Scatter with the rest of the cheese and bake in the preheated oven for 15–18 minutes until golden.

croutons etc.

Croutons add a much-needed contrast of crunch to creamy or puréed soups. A simple Spiced Carrot (page 77) or Leek and Potato Soup (page 57) are ideal candidates for a scattering of croutons. But really you can scatter them on anything you like.

baked croutons

⅓ cup plus 1 tablespoon extra virgin olive oil

1 garlic clove, crushed

1 small baguette or ½ large baguette, cut into ¾-inch cubes

3½ oz Gruyère cheese or Parmesan (optional)

makes 15–20

Preheat the oven to 400˚F.

Mix the oil and garlic together and season well. Place the baguette on a baking sheet and brush with the oil. If you'd like cheesy croutons, scatter over the cheese. Bake in the preheated oven for 20–25 minutes until crisp and golden.

fried garlic croutons

The best croutons are fried. Any leftovers work well with a simple watercress salad with a poached egg, or with chunks of avocado and fried bacon. They are a must for the humble Chicken Avgolemono (page 14) and since they are so garlicky and lovely, they go well with the Mediterranean tomato-based soups.

6 tablespoons extra virgin olive oil

3 slices of stale white bread, ¾ inch thick (crusts cut off), cut into ¾-inch cubes

4 whole garlic cloves, unpeeled

makes 30–40

Heat the olive oil in a large skillet until a bread cube sizzles and turns brown in 4 seconds. Add the bread and garlic. Cook, stirring constantly, over medium heat for 2 minutes, or until golden brown. Discard the garlic cloves and drain the croutons on paper towels.

chile and sesame pita toasts

These are great for scooping up chunky soups and particularly good with bean-based soups. If you have any left over a tub of hummus and a handful of these work wonders for a midafternoon snack.

2 garlic cloves, crushed

6 tablespoons extra virgin olive oil

½ teaspoon ground red pepper

1 tablespoon sesame seeds

4 pita breads

makes 32

Preheat the oven to 350°F.

Combine the garlic, olive oil, red pepper, and sesame seeds in a bowl and season with sea salt. Cut each pita into 4 strips and separate each one into a single layer. Place, split-side up, on a baking sheet and brush with the oil mixture. Bake in the preheated oven for 10–15 minutes until crisp and lightly golden.

Let cool for 5 minutes and store in an airtight container for up to 3 days.

Taleggio and sage focaccia rolls

This is very much like batch-baking bread rolls. You make individual swirly rolls, like cinnamon buns, then push them into a pan together, so you can break them off as you want to eat them and they stay soft on the inside. Make sure you line the baking pan or the cheese will burn onto the pan.

2 cups bread flour

2 teaspoons active dry yeast

1 teaspoon sugar

1 teaspoon salt

⅔ cup milk, warmed

¼ cup extra virgin olive oil

10 oz Taleggio cheese
(rind cut off), cubed

a handful of fresh sage leaves,
roughly chopped

1 tablespoon coarse salt

freshly ground black pepper

*an 8-inch square baking pan,
lined with parchment paper*

makes 9

Put the flour in a food mixer with a dough hook, or in a mixing bowl.

In a separate bowl, mix together the yeast, sugar, and salt and 3 tablespoons of the warm milk. Add the yeast mixture to the flour and start to mix, adding enough of the remaining milk and the olive oil to create a soft but not too sticky dough. If using a mixer, knead for 8 minutes. Alternatively, knead by hand on a lightly floured surface for 15 minutes until smooth and elastic. Put the dough in a clean bowl, cover, and leave in a warm, draft-free place for 30 minutes, or until doubled in size.

Roll the dough out on a lightly floured surface into a rectangle approximately 12 x 8 inches. Scatter with the cheese and most of the sage. Season with freshly ground black pepper. Roll up from the long side to cover all the cheese and sit on its seam. Cut into 1¼-inch slices—you should get 9 swirly rolls. Arrange these in the baking pan. Scatter with the reserved sage and the coarse salt, cover the pan with plastic wrap, and let rise for 30 minutes.

Preheat the oven to 400°F.

Bake in the preheated oven for 25 minutes, or until golden and cooked through.

red bell pepper scones

The secret with scones is just to make them nice and thick.
Serve these warm with butter—they are irresistible.

1¾ cups self-rising flour

3 tablespoons butter, diced

1 teaspoon baking powder

1 tablespoon freshly chopped
rosemary, plus 10 small sprigs

3½ oz roasted red bell peppers,
drained and finely chopped

1 egg

3 tablespoons milk, plus extra
to glaze

makes 10–12

Preheat the oven to 425°F.

Mix the flour and butter in a food processor or with
your fingertips until it resembles crumbs. Mix in the
baking powder, chopped rosemary, a pinch of salt, and
the peppers. Beat the egg with the milk, then pour into
the flour, stirring with a knife until you have a smooth
dough. Roll out the dough on a lightly floured surface
so it is at least ¾ inch thick and cut out 2-inch circles.
Keep rerolling until you have 10–12 scones. Push the
rosemary sprigs into the tops, place on a baking sheet,
brush with milk, and bake for 15 minutes until golden.

cornbread muffins

Cornbread made with stone-ground cornmeal is a real treat
and it's easy because there's no need to bother with yeast.

2 green chiles, seeded

1 cup stone-ground cornmeal

½ cup grated Parmesan

1½ cups all-purpose flour

1 tablespoon baking powder

2 tablespoons sugar

½ teaspoon cayenne pepper

1 egg, beaten

5 tablespoons butter, melted

1 generous cup buttermilk

3–5 tablespoons whole milk

a muffin pan, greased

makes 9

Preheat the oven to 350°F.

Chop the chiles and mix with the cornmeal, Parmesan,
flour, baking powder, sugar, cayenne, and a large pinch
of salt. In a large measuring cup beat the egg, butter,
and buttermilk. Stir the wet ingredients into the dry
ingredients until there are no more floury pockets and
add enough milk so that it becomes wet. It won't be of
pouring consistency and will have to be dolloped into
the muffin pan. Don't overbeat it or you'll make the
mixture tough. Spoon into the muffin pan and bake for
30 minutes until golden.

zucchini, lemon thyme, and feta loaf

This is a cross between a savory bread and a cake. It doesn't need proofing or kneading—it rises with baking powder a bit like soda bread, so it's super simple to prepare. I love it on a hot day with gazpacho or on a cold evening I toast it, slather it with butter, and serve it with any of the more Mediterranean or Middle Eastern soups.

2½ cups all-purpose flour

2 tablespoons baking powder

1 teaspoon salt

¾ cup plus 2 tablespoons whole milk

⅔ cup extra virgin olive oil

2 eggs, beaten

1 large zucchini, coarsely grated

4 oz feta, crumbled

2 fresh lemon thyme sprigs, leaves only

freshly ground black pepper

a 9 x 5 x 3-inch loaf pan, lined with parchment paper

makes a large loaf

Preheat the oven to 350°F.

Sift the flour, baking powder, and salt into a large bowl and season with freshly ground black pepper.

In a large measuring cup, combine the milk and olive oil and beat in the eggs. Stir into the dry ingredients along with the zucchini, two-thirds of the feta, and half the thyme leaves. Stir until there are no more floury pockets but don't overbeat it or you'll make the mixture tough. Spoon into the prepared loaf pan. Scatter over the remaining feta and remaining thyme. Bake in the preheated oven for 1–1¼ hours, or until a skewer inserted in the center comes out clean.

Remove from the oven and let cool for 10 minutes in the loaf pan, then turn out onto a wire rack to cool completely.

index

conversion charts

Weights and measures have been rounded up or down slightly to make measuring easier.

Volume equivalents:

American	Metric	Imperial
1 teaspoon	5 ml	
1 tablespoon	15 ml	
¼ cup	60 ml	2 fl oz
⅓ cup	75 ml	2½ fl oz
½ cup	125 ml	4 fl oz
⅔ cup	150 ml	5 fl oz (¼ pint)
¾ cup	175 ml	6 fl oz
1 cup	250 ml	8 fl oz

Weight equivalents: Measurements:

Imperial	Metric	Inches	cm
1 oz	25 g	¼ inch	5 mm
2 oz	50 g	½ inch	1 cm
3 oz	75 g	¾ inch	1.5 cm
4 oz	125 g	1 inch	2.5 cm
5 oz	150 g	2 inches	5 cm
6 oz.	175 g	3 inches	7 cm
7 oz	200 g	4 inches	10 cm
8 oz (½ lb)	250 g	5 inches	12 cm
9 oz	275 g	6 inches	15 cm
10 oz	300 g	7 inches	18 cm
11 oz	325 g	8 inches	20 cm
12 oz	375 g	9 inches	23 cm
13 oz	400 g	10 inches	25 cm
14 oz	425 g	11 inches	28 cm
15 oz	475 g	12 inches	30 cm
16 oz (1 lb)	500 g		
2 lb	1 kg		

1 stick of butter is roughly equivalent to 4 oz or 115 g

Oven temperatures:

110°C	(225°F)	Gas ¼
120°C	(250°F)	Gas ½
140°C	(275°F)	Gas 1
150°C	(300°F)	Gas 2
160°C	(325°F)	Gas 3
180°C	(350°F)	Gas 4
190°C	(375°F)	Gas 5
200°C	(400°F)	Gas 6
220°C	(425°F)	Gas 7
230°C	(450°F)	Gas 8
240°C	(475°F)	Gas 9